C000049796

The Ultimate Sacrifice
The World War II Battleship

by

David Turner

Published by

MELROSE BOOKS

An Imprint of Melrose Press
St Thomas Place, Ely
Cambridgeshire
CB7 4GG, UK
www.melrosebooks.co.uk

FIRST EDITION

Copyright © David Turner 2004

The Author asserts his moral right to
be identified as the author of this work

Cover illustration by Bryan Carpenter

ISBN 0 95484801 2

All rights reserved. No Part of this publication may be reproduced, stored in a retrieval system, or transmitted, in any form or by any means electronic, mechanical, photocopying, recording or otherwise, without the prior permission of the publishers.

This book is sold subject to the condition that it shall not, by way of trade or otherwise, be lent, re-sold, hired out or otherwise circulated without the publisher's prior consent in any form of binding or cover other than that in which it is published and without a similar condition including this condition being imposed on the subsequent purchaser.

Printed and bound in Great Britain by:
Antony Rowe, Bumper's Farm Industrial Estate
Chippenham, Wiltshire, SN14 6LH, UK

They shall not grow old, as we that
are left grow old:
Age shall not weary them, nor
the years condemn.
At the going down of the sun,
and in the morning,
We will remember them.

Laurence Binyon

In Memory of my Late Uncle

Commander Ralph Lennox Woodrow-Clark RN

1905-1939

**This book is also dedicated to
the many officers and men who lost their lives;
the survivors; and their families and relatives.**

Foreword

The mighty squadrons of dreadnoughts epitomized naval power even after the disasters that showed how vulnerable they could be.

A Nation's strength was often determined by the number of its battleships. The aircraft carrier, a despised rival, usurped the position of a battleship as a capital ship within months of the outbreak of World War II.

The battleships *Royal Oak*, *Prince of Wales* and *Repulse* had been sunk.

Launching of the *Royal Oak* – HM Dockyard Devonport – By Viscountess Vallatort with Mr Hockaday (Manager of Construction, Devonport Dockyard) and Admiral Manday

Chaplains service prior to launching *Royal Oak* in 1914

Photographs courtesy of the Plymouth Naval Base Museum

A Nation at War

In June 1939, after a visit to Torbay, the Royal Oak sailed into Devonport, her birthplace, where the crew were issued with tropical clothing in the belief they were going to the Mediterranean. However, as the Second World War seemed inevitable, the Royal Oak was ordered to sail to Scapa Flow in the Orkney Islands.

At 11:15am on 3rd September 1939, Prime Minister Chamberlain made a sad and uninspired broadcast to tell the nation they were at war.

On the evening of September 15th 1939, Churchill boarded a London train with Lieutenant Commander C.R ('Tommy') Thompson, the first Lord's Flag Commander. Their destination was off the north coast of Scotland: the anchorage of Britain's home fleet in the sea basin of Scapa Flow. There, if anywhere, Churchill thought, the Royal Navy should be buttoned up. Later, he recalled how "on two or three occasions" in the autumn of 1914, most memorably on October 17th, "The alarm was given that there was a U-boat inside the anchorage. Guns were fired, destroyers thrashed the waters, and the whole gigantic armada put out to sea in haste and dudgeon", Scapa was that important.

Anxiety over the sea basin had returned, and this time the threat was real. In Churchill's lap lay a locked box of secret documents, among them a shocking report from the Chiefs of Staff Committee revealing that Scapa's defences would not be ready until the spring of 1940. Upon arrival he called on Sir Charles Forbes, the Commander in Chief, aboard HMS Nelson, the Admiral's flagship. Sir Charles confirmed that the basin's entrance channels were "not properly netted". The old steel webs had rusted, rotted, broken up, and drifted away. Churchill immediately issued an order, stamped 'urgent', calling for nets, booms, blockships (sunken ships barring entrance channels), anti-aircraft guns, patrol craft, balloons and searchlights. Until they were in place, Scapa was insecure, an inviting target for daring German submarine commanders.

U-boat Kapitäns, so successful in sinking merchant ships were now turning their periscopes towards Britain's ships of war. It was disquieting to know that Dönitz's vessels were lurking in British waters, capable of striking one of his Majesty's capital ships at any hour. Churchill's anxiety over Scapa Flow continued.

It is well known that two U-boats had attempted to penetrate the deep, almost landlocked, basin in the First World War and neither had returned, but, studying aerial photographs of the anchorage in 1939, Dönitz reached the conclusion that an adroit navigator could thread his way past the three sunken ships meant to block Holm Sound.

Prien was his best U-boat Kapitän, and he almost failed. It took him nearly six hours to do it – at one point he seemed hopelessly ensnared in a cable from one of the block-ships. The story of this maritime tragedy is described within the following pages.

Ralph Lennox Woodrow-Clark – killed in action

It was a dark and cold winter evening on October 14th 1939. I was nine years old and had arrived home from school to find my mother crying in the kitchen of our house at Laira in Plymouth.

When I asked "Why are you crying Mummy?" she told me that the BBC Home Service had reported late that morning an announcement by the Secretary to the Admiralty:

"It is with regret that I have to announce that the battleship *HMS Royal Oak* has been sunk, it is believed by U-boat action, fifteen survivors have been landed"

My uncle, Ralph Lennox Woodrow-Clark, my mother's elder brother, was a senior officer on board the *Royal Oak* when she was torpedoed and sunk at Scapa Flow on October 14th 1939. It was to be a further five days before the sea 'gave up' my uncle.

His grave is in the Lyness Royal Navy Cemetery on the island of Hoy between Mill Bay and Ore Bay.

Educated at the Royal Naval Colleges of Dartmouth and Greenwich, his future had promised promotion to the highest ranks within the Royal Navy.

I made a promise to mother that one day I would visit his last resting place. It was to be a further 64 years before I was able to fulfill that promise.

The untimely death of my uncle became even more harrowing to his family and friends when it was known that he had been promoted to the rank of Commander and was due to take up a new post in one of His Majesty's Royal Navy capital ships.

David Turner

Fact, Fiction, Bad Communication

Churchill was informed immediately of the sinking of the *Royal Oak* and the loss of 833 officers and men, among them Captain W.G Benn and Rear Admiral H.E.C. Blagrove (Commander of the 2nd Battle Squadron).

When told, Churchill said, "Poor fellows, poor fellows, trapped in those black depths".
He wept, then thought of the unknown submariners' achievement and murmured "what a wonderful feat of arms".

Rear Admiral Blagrove, after refusing a lifebuoy offered to him by a crew member of *Daisy II*, spent the last few minutes of his life helping others.

The sinking of the *Royal Oak* was one of the biggest disasters of the Second World War.

At a subsequent Admiralty Board of Enquiry, Captain Benn was called to give evidence about the tragedy. Due to bad communication, Churchill had been told, in error, that the captain was lost with the ship.

British Battleship Losses 1939–1945

HMS Royal Oak	14th October 1939	Torpedoed, Scapa Flow by U-47
HMS Hood	24th May 1941	Destroyed in *Bismarck* action
HMS Barham	25th November 1941	Torpedoed, Mediterranean by U331
HMS Prince of Wales	10th December 1941	Air attack, Malaya
HMS Repulse	10th December 1941	Air attack, Malaya

As the most expensive and advanced ships of their time, battleships could only be built by the leading nations, and the threat of a battleship's guns was a potent political instrument.

HMS Warspite, Flagship of the Mediterranean Fleet, was probably the most famous British battleship of World War II.

The British followed the strategy that had proved so successful in World War I, moving the home fleet to Scapa Flow to block the exits to the Atlantic. However, this time the great fleet base did not prove immune to attack.

Admiralty Projections for New Battleships in 1920

Quantity	Type	Tonnage	Number and Size of Guns	Top Speed
4	Hood Class	41,200 tons	8 x 15 inch	31 knots
2	Repulse	27,000 tons	6 x 15 inch	31 knots
5	Revenge	29,150 tons	8 x 15 inch	22 knots
5	Queen Elizabeth	27,500 tons	8 x 15 inch	24 knots
4	Iron Duke	25,000 tons	10 x 13.5 inch	21 knots
3	King George V	23,000 tons	10 x 13.5 inch	21 knots
4	Orion	22,000 tons	10 x 13.5 inch	21 knots
1	Tiger	28,500 tons	8 x 13.5 inch	30 knots

Projections for new battleships provided a distinctly bleak outlook. For, although on paper they had an enormous superiority in numbers, the older dreadnoughts were weakly armed and protected in comparison with the new Japanese and American battleships.

The British Hood design was a follow-on from the Queen Elizabeth design, a fast battleship rather than a battle-cruiser with 12-inch armour and a speed of 31 knots. Although she incorporated many new features such as inclined armour, her design was too far advanced for all the lessons of Jutland to be incorporated and, as a result, her deck protection was not adequate against long-range shell-fire. The Director of Naval Construction regarded the design as inadequate in the light of wartime experience. The Admiralty, therefore, gave up all thought of completing work on the three modified sisters of the *Hood.*

The Admiralty had hoped to order three new 43,500 ton battleships armed with nine 18-inch guns and a 48,000 ton battle-cruiser with nine 16-inch guns in the 1921-1922 financial year, and the same number of ships the following year. However, the existing battle-cruisers were so weakly protected that the Board revised the programme to four battle-cruisers in the 1921-1922 programme and four battleships to follow in 1922-1923.

Royal Oak

The *Royal Oak* is a war grave. The sinking of the *Royal Oak* during the early weeks of the Second World War was a national disaster. Although she was over 25 years old, the battleship was considered to be robust and strong enough to resist enemy attack. This faith proved to be unwarranted.

The battleship *HMS Royal Oak* at anchor

The *Royal Oak* was the last and largest battleship to be built at Devonport between 1914 and 1916. She was nearly 600ft long with a maximum width of 100 ft. She was armed with eight 15 inch guns contained in four turrets, plus an assemblage of twelve 6-inch guns, eight 4-inch anti-aircraft guns and four 21-inch torpedo tubes. The warship was well armoured with 13 inches of steel that extended 5ft below her water line. She was capable of 20 knots at top speed powered by 40,000 horsepower oil-fuelled engines. A crew of nearly 1100 men was needed to handle her. She saw action at the Battle of Jutland.

After the outbreak of war, German reconnaissance aircraft took photographs over Scapa Flow of British ships at anchor and the state of the harbour defences. These were passed to Kommodore Karl Dönitz, commodore of the Unterseeboote arm of the Kriegsmarine, ultimately to become an admiral, Deputy Führer, and for a brief time, Führer. After studying the photographs and reports, Dönitz decided that, given the right man, a U-boat could attack [illegible] opportunity was given to Kapitän-leutnant Günther Prien to command the VHB type U-boat, *U-47*.

Royal naval divers visit the wreck annually to carry out a survey and replace the white ensign, hoisting it under water. A moving memorial service and wreath-laying ceremony is also conducted near the site every year on the Saturday falling closest to the anniversary of her sinking. The remaining survivors and their families gather together at the Naval War Memorial on Southsea Common at her home base of Portsmouth to hold a service in memory of those who went down with this mighty battleship. The survivors, relatives and Orcadians all remember and respect. So must we all.

***HMS Royal Oak* in Portsmouth Harbour before the start of World War Two**

Scapa Flow

At the heart of the Orkney Islands off Britain's north coast lies the great open stretch of sea known as Scapa Flow. This vast basin, 10 miles across at its widest point, forms a natural harbour between the North Sea to the east and the Atlantic Ocean to the west. The broken concrete that can still be seen in these islands bears witness to Scapa Flow's importance as the main naval base for the British Home Fleet in two world wars.

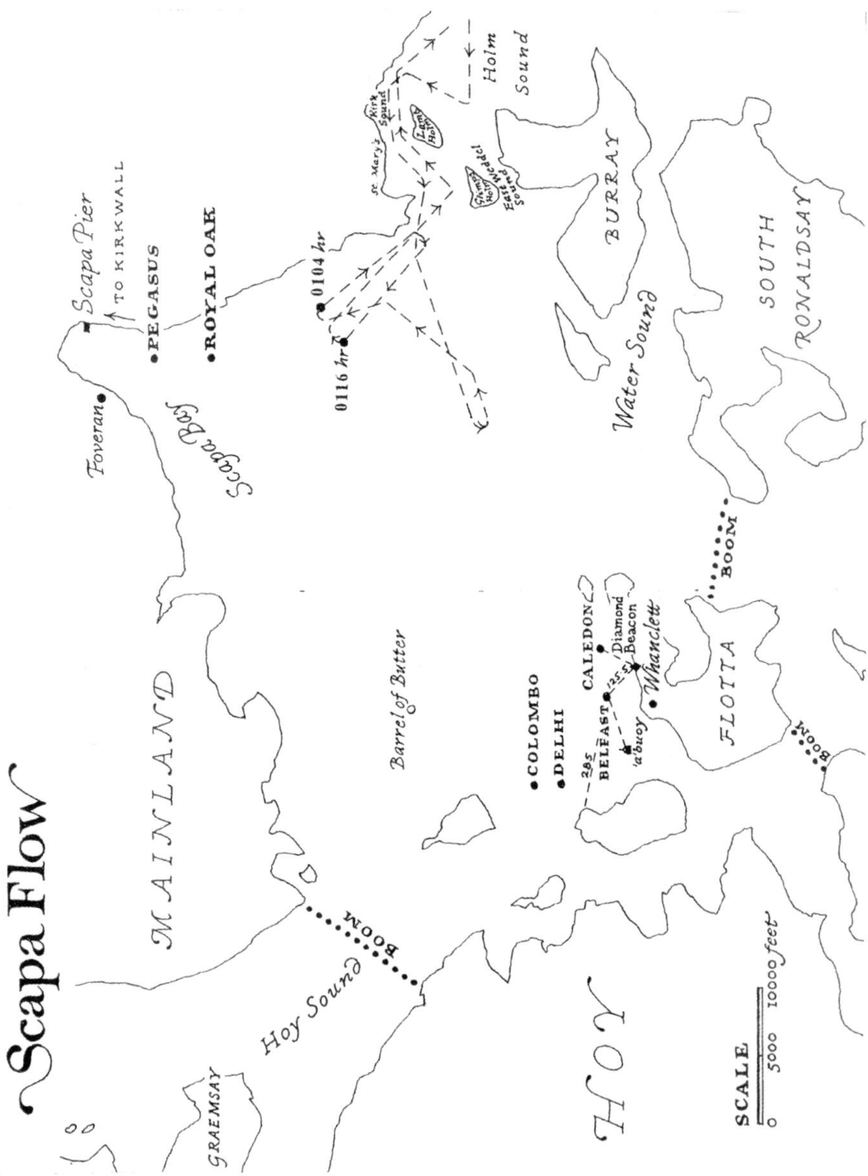
Scapa Flow
MAINLAND
GRAEMSAY
Hoy Sound
BOOM
HOY
SCALE
0 5000 10000 feet
Barrel of Butter
COLOMBO
DELHI
BELFAST
CALEDON
'a' buoy
Diamond Beacon
Whanclett
FLOTTA
BOOM
BOOM
Water Sound
SOUTH RONALDSAY
BURRAY
Scapa Bay
Foveran
Scapa Pier
TO KIRKWALL
PEGASUS
ROYAL OAK
0104 hr
0116 hr
St. Mary's
Kirk Sound
Lamb Holm
Glims Holm
Weddel
East Weddel Sound
Holm Sound

***U-47* leaves Kiel for Scapa Flow, 8th October 1939**

The German U-boat *U-47* sailed from her base at Kiel on Sunday 8th October 1939 – destination Scapa Flow! On that day, the *Royal Oak,* accompanied by two screening destroyers, was patrolling the channel between Fair Isle and Orkney. Her mission was to prevent the German battlecruiser *Gneisenau* from breaking into the Atlantic and attacking the merchant convoys that supplied Britain.

The *Gneisenau* had been reported off Norway and the British battle-cruisers *Hood* and *Repulse*, together with the newest battleships, *Nelson* and *Rodney*, and the aircraft carrier *Furious*, with scouting and screening destroyers, had set off across the North Sea to intercept her, leaving *Royal Oak* to close the gap between Orkney and Shetland. There were tremendous gales during the next day or so and even a ship the size of *Royal Oak* suffered in the violent seas. Massive waves swept along her forecastle deck, damaging fittings and carrying away Carley life rafts, with water severely flooding the battery deck. The *Royal Oak* was ordered back to port and arrived back in Scapa Flow on October 11th. Rather than leave the capital ships in Scapa Flow they were sent away to protect them from Luftwaffe attacks.

The *Royal Oak* was ordered to the north-east of the anchorage where her anti-aircraft guns could protect the important radio direction-finding station at Netherbutton, near Kirkwall.

As the *U-47* continued its mission to penetrate Scapa Flow, the crew of the *Royal Oak* spent Friday 13th October clearing up the shambles below decks after her rough passage earlier in the week. She also took stores on board.

All that day, the [illegible] North Sea, 90 metres down, some miles to the east of the Orkney Islands.

On the nights of 13th and 14th October 1939, the *U-47* under Kapitän-leutnant Günther Prien penetrated the line of block ships in Kirk Sound and found the old battleship *Royal Oak* lying at anchor before him, bows to the north-east along both the direction of wind and the eddy current set up in Scapa Bay by the ebbing tide.

Prien's first salvo of three torpedoes fired from ahead failed to do any damage, for the one torpedo that did hit apparently struck an anchor chain or detonated only partially.

After an interval to reload, Prien fired another salvo and this time there was a loud explosion underneath the *Royal Oak* and she rolled over and sank within minutes. By 01:30, all that was to be seen of the *Royal Oak* was fuel oil and men desperately fighting for their lives. A total of 833 men died with her.

It has been said that she was destroyed by a colossal explosion, but Admiralty records show only that the ship capsized and sank after heavy flooding amidships. The loss of 24 officers and 809 men was much greater than it need have been because the ship's company had not yet become accustomed to war routine.

No doubt feeling secure in a quiet corner of the anchorage, the ship's officers had not ensured that all the watertight doors and hatches were closed and so the ship was at her most vulnerable. The *Royal Oak* was only fit for second-line duties, but the skill of Prien and his *U-47* in penetrating a base that had been thought to be impregnable shook the confidence of the Admiralty and infuriated Churchill.

As in 1914, the Home Fleet had been sent away to bases on the West Coast of Scotland until the defences could be strengthened.

The Royal Navy reacted quickly. On the 15th October, nets were spread over the wreck to catch any floating bodies. Divers went down to inspect the wreck. Some ascended in horror at the sight of the suspended bodies that they encountered.

Men were found jammed in the portholes as they tried in desperation to get out of the wreck. The decision was taken immediately to place three further block ships in Kirk Sound.

It was not then known how *U-47* had got in, and this action demonstrated that the precise weaknesses in the defences had been recognised even before the *Royal Oak* tragedy.

Churchill ordered the construction of barriers. The Churchill barriers, as they were named, were sufficiently high in 1942 to prevent any repetition of the *Royal Oak* incident. They were completed in 1944.

The attack infuriated Churchill

The following detailed account does not appear in the Admiralty records, and is as recounted to the author by an unknown survivor of the tragedy, who wishes to remain anonymous.

A torpedo from the *U-47* scored a direct hit on the *Royal Oak*'s starboard side, another torpedo started a fire in the magazine, while yet another blew a huge hole in the engine room. Almost immediately, the mighty battleship that had fought at the Battle of Jutland in 1916 keeled over 45 degrees and went to the sea-bed. The inferno on board destroyed the crowded mess decks, taking a heavy toll of boy seamen, ratings and Royal Marines: some, burned and suffering from shock, ran through flames to jump into the sea. Down below, in the confined machinery spaces and boiler room, stokers fought blindly to escape the choking smoke and scalding steam, but many of the steel ladders had buckled in the intense heat preventing the men from escaping.

At 02:15, the *U-47* slipped out of Scapa Flow and headed for home, reaching [illegible] 17th October 1939 at 11:44. They were given a heroes welcome and the entire crew was flown to Berlin to be greeted [illegible] Hitler.

The Royal Navy at its mightiest: the 2nd Battle Squadron seen from beneath the 15-inch guns of *HMS Royal Oak*

The Ultimate Sacrifice

A partial list of names of men lost after *HMS Royal Oak* was sunk in 1939. In total 833 lives were lost and all are included in a final roll-call available for all to see in St Magnus Cathedral, Kirkwall, Orkney, and at the Scapa Flow Visitor Centre and Museum, Lyness, Orkney. *By kind permission of The Daily Telegraph.*

Abbot , S.E.
Ackerman, A.G.
Adams, W.P.
Agnew, C.W.
Alberry, J.
Allen, A.F.
Allen, P.L.
Amos, E.J.
Anderson, E.
Anderson, H.L.
Anderson, R.F.
Anderson, W.B.
Anderson, W.T.
Andrews, E.H.
Andrews, G.C.
Andrews W.E.
Annell, F.W.
Armfield, L.
Armitage, F.C.
Armstrong, G.H.
Arno, R.
Ashby, K.
Ashwin, A.W.
Atherton, J.
Atherton, N.
Atkinson, J.
Atkinson, T.E.
Attard, F.
Attard, L.
Attfield, H.G.
Azzopardi, A.
Baigent, G.H.
Bailey, C.W.
Bailey, E.R.
Bain, R.
Baker, A.E.
Baker, A.W.
Baker, W.G.M.
Baldwin, A.S.
Ball, R.J.
Ballard, E.F.
Balls, H.E.
Barber, A.S.
Barber, F.
Bargery, A.E.
Barker, E.H.
Barnes-Moss, H.W.
Barnfather, R.N.
Bartlett, A.
Bartolo, J.
Bealing, F.C.
Beange, J.
Beddall, H.
Bedwell, H.
Beechy, A.C.
Beer, A.E.
Bell, R.W.
Bendall, R.F.J.
Bennett, W.
Benney, C.E.
Beswick, H.W.J.
Betts, H.J.
Betts, W.T.
[illegible]
Binns, F.B.
Binsley, G.F.
Birtchnell, C.E.
Black, J.

Blackborough, J.W.
Blagrove, H.E.C.
Blenkiron, N.
Blood, S.
Blyth, H.B.
Boening, J.
Bold, P.W.
Bonello, S.
Bonner, W.C.
Borland, D.A.
Bottomley, R.J.
Bowden, R.C.
Bowen, J.
Bowhay, W.J.R.
Boyd, T.A.
Boyes, L.S.
Boyle, W.
Brading, C.E.
Bradwick, A.H.
Bramley, R.J.
Branch, H.
Bridges, J.G.C.
Bright, H.
Brightman, G.R.
Briscoe, E.
Britton, T.F.
Brookin, J.F.
Broughton, A.E.
Brown, A.G.
Brown, D.A.J.
Brown, H.
Brown, H.W.
Brown, J.
Brymer, E.A.
Buckett, S.V.
Bucknall, A.G.
Budge, J.
Bull, A.N.
Burden, A.E.
Burnham, P.
Burns, A.
Burns, J.E.
Burrows, R.W.
Burt, E.H.
Burtenshaw, C.H.
Burton, J.W.
Butler, A.A.
Butler, A.E.
Butler, A.E.
Bydawell, L.R.J.
Cachia, J.
Cairns, J.
Campbell, C.H.
Campbell, D.
Campsie, C.
Cannon, R.J.
Capel, C.W.
Card, A.R.W.
Carnegie, A.K.
Carpenter, E.G.
Carr, F.C.
Carter, G.W.
Carter, J.
[illegible]
Cartwright, W.
Cass, L.
Cast, R.I.
Chadwick, J.C.

Chadwick, T.
Chalk, R.G.
Callenger, A.L.
Chappell, W.G.
Cheesley, W.H.G.
Chesman, W.E.
Chick, A.
Church, O.
Clacher, W.H.
Clackson, R.G.
Clark, A.H.
Clark, A.J.
Clark, F.H.
Clark, J.
Clark, R.L.W.
Clarke, F.H.
Clarke, R.E.
Clements, E.F.J.
Clementson, J.
Cloute, E.C.
Cock, C.H.
Coffin, L.J.
Colbourne, F.E.
Colbourne, J.W.F
Colbran, P.B.
Coleman, E.W.
Coleman, J.A.
Coleman, M.G.N.
Collins, G.A.
Collins, R.
Comber, A.E.B.
Connor, F.
Connor, R.J.
Conroy, F.
Cook, G.J.
Cooke, F.A.
Cooper, L.L.
Cooper, N.
Cope, J.R.
Coreschi, E.
Cornelious, K.T.
Cornelius, H.J.
Cornish, C.F.
Cousins, H.J.
Cox, E.
Cragg, W.
Craven, A.
Cree, J.D.B.
Crockett, J.S.
Crofts, E.A.
Cross, E.V.A.
Crosswell, W.H.
Cumbes, R.W.
Cumming, L.T.J.
Cummings, H.
Cunningham, E.W.
Curtin, C.
Curtis, H.H.W.
Cutler, J.A.
Daniels, G.
Darnell, G.T.
Daughtrey, A.
Davey, C.B.
[illegible]
Davies, M.C.
Davis, J.F.
Davis, R.E.
Dayish A.

Deacon, W.J.
Dear, A.J.
Deighton, E.C.
Derbyshire, R.
Derry, J.O.H.
Diaper, S.T.
Dickie, W.A.
Doe, S.P.
Doggett, I.E.
Dowding, P.W.G.
Downes, A.F.
Draper, B.H.
Druce, A.
Duncalf, T.
Dunk, C.A.
Dunk, W.W.
Dyer, H.
Eade, J.H.
Easton, F.
Ede, F.
Edwards, A.
Edwards, J.F.
Edwards, R.G.
Edwards, W.R.A.
Efemey, R.B.
Elliott, R.
Eltringham, N.
Emery, A.
Emery, F.C.
Evans, B.
Evans, J.E.
Eyers, C.E.
Fairbrother, J.W.
Farr, E.W.
Farrell, R.
Fenn, T.R.P.
Finlay, M.B.
Fisher, B.L.
Fisher, J.B.
Fitch, C.E.
Flogdell, A.E.
Flounders, A.
Ford, W.J.
Forsey, H.S.
Foster, D.C.
Foster, G.W.
Foulger, A.
Fowler, J.W.
Foyle, A.A.
Francis, H.A.
Franckeiss, E.L.
French, C.
Fuller, C.W.
Furbear, T.G.
Furby, E.A.
Furlong, J.
Furnell, L.T.
Gallagher, J.W.
Gibbons, J.A.
Gibson, G.
Gibson, S.J.
Gile, W.H.
Gill, G.E.
Gill, H.W.
[illegible]
Godley, S.G.
Godwin, T.G.
Godwin, W.

Golding, A.
Goodyear, J.C.
Goorlay, J.R.G.
Gorsuch, E.D.
Gough, E.J.
Gough, T.E.
Gowan, J.D.
Grace, V.M.
Graham, G.M.
Graham, P.W.C.
Graham, S.
Graham-Brown, J.L.T.
Gray, A.
Gray, E.
Gray, H.W.
Grech, J.
Green, F.
Green, F.A.
Green, R.
Greenwood, L.
Griffin, H.
Griffiths, E.J.
Griffiths, J.R.
Grindey, A.E.
Grogan, J.
Giusti, I.
Gutteridge, R.G.N.
Guy, R.
Hales, J.
Hall, H.J.
Hall, J.
Hall, K.E.
Hall, W.R.
Hamblin, G.A.
Hamblin, H.J.
Hammond, J.S.
Hammond, W.L.
Hance, T.R.
Harkin, P.R.
Harle, G.
Harley, J.A.H.
Harper, R.R.J.
Harris, G.J.
Harris, K.J.
Harris, N.H.
Harris, P.W.
Hawkins, K.R.J.
Hawkins, W.J.
Hayes, T.
Hayward, J.G.
Heather, C.W.
Helmore, W.L.
Hemestretch, C.W.
Hemsley, C.F.
Henstridge, C.
Heslop, C.
Hicks, A.E.
Higgins, J.J.
Higgs, H.H.
Highfield, J.E.
Hill, A.
Hill, D.
Hill, D.
Hill, E.F.
[illegible]
Hingston, E.
Hiscock, F.J.
Hixson, H.H.

Hocking, J.R.
Hodgson, A.R.
Hodgson, J.S.
Hodson, F.H.J.
Holland, C.
Holyoak, E.
Hotton, L.W.T.
Hudson, J.C.
Huggins, H.S.
Hughes, F.E.
Hughes, T.
Hughes-Rowlands, R.
Hull, E.C.
Hull, R.G.
Humber, J.F.
Hunt, A.V.
Hunt, E.G.
Hunter, F.
Hunter, J.
Hurst, F.
Huscroft, R.W.
Hussey-Yeo, A.J.
Hutchcocks, T.
Hyde, A.J.
Hyde, G.M.
Ing, R.
Jack, J.D.
Jackman, J.J.
Jackson, L.T.D.
Jackson, T.W.
Jacobs, W.A.C.
Jago, L.
James, L.J.
James, R.
James, V.L.
Jay, V.G.U.
Jelley, L.J.
Jenkins, E.J.A.
Jenkins, T.S.
Jennings, R.E.
Jewell, A.
Jewer, S.A.
Jobson, J.B.
Johns, P.H.M.
Johnson, F.W.P.
Johnson, T.W.
Johnston, A.J.
Jones, C.E.
Jones, H.
Jones, H.G.
Jones, S.
Jones, T.J.
Jordon, F.
Jordon, H.D.
Judge, P.R.
Kane, R.C.
Kearey, A.
Keel, J.
Keel, W.
Kemp, L.H.
Kempster, A.
Kennedy, R.H.
Kennedy, W.T.
Kennett, E.H.
[illegible]
Kersey, H.A.
Kidby, W.F.
King, C.E.M

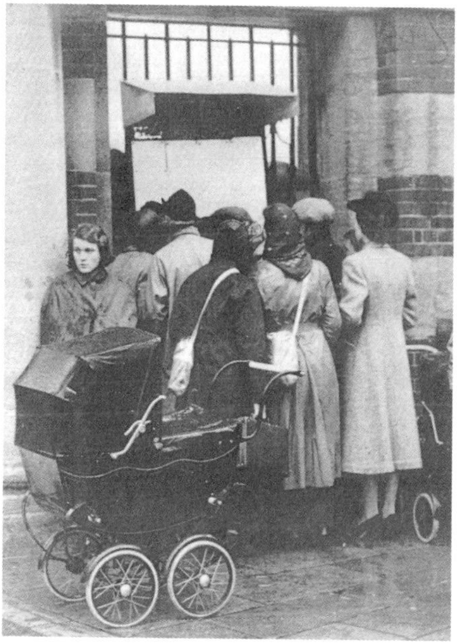

The families of those serving on *HMS Royal Oak* hunt for names on the list of survivors: 833 officers and men were lost with the ship

THE DAILY TELEGRAPH

MONDAY, OCTOBER 16, 1939

H.M.S. ROYAL OAK SURVIVORS

8 LISTS ISSUED BY THE ADMIRALTY

The names of survivors of H.M.S. Royal Oak, as far as they were known on Saturday, were issued at intervals during the day.

There were seven lists, containing 396 names, and yesterday an eighth list, containing 18 names, was issued.

The lists are as follows:

FIRST LIST

Lt. A. M. Seymour, Pay. Cadet M. Holligan, Wt. Eng. G. Dunstone.

P.O. P. Higgins, J 102348; P.O. E. A. Rowland, JX 129913; AB C. B. McCabe, SX 16346; L.S. A. Harmer, PJ. 111268; O.S. E. Smith, PSSX 26107; O.S. Crichton, PSSX 27417; O.S. R. Martin, JX 157051; Boy R. W. Scovell, JX 155206; Chief Stoker C. Hine, PK 57468; Stoker H. P. Cleverly, PKX 95939; Cook G. R. States, P 55424; Marine J. W. Woods, POX 2320.

SECOND LIST

Lt. G. O. Roberts; Wt. Shipwright W. E. Harding; Cmd Gunner J. T. Pearce.

P.O. J. R. Kerr, P/J 98827; L.S. H. J. Instance, P/JX 139683; A.B. William Hancox, P/SSX 19677; A.B. Alfred Elmes, P/J 97246; A.B. John Ross, R.N.R., 193628; O.S. V. Marchant, P/SSX 26198; Boy David Belben, P/JX 158176; Boy Jack Bromyard P/JX 159377; Yeo. Sigs. William C. Mitchell, P/J 102472; Stoker William Tate, P/KX 89315; Stoker Oswald L. Fletcher.

Ord. Art. Hector Randell, P/M 47990; Ord. Art. Edward Dommett; E.R.A. 5th Class Brocker, P/MX 51638; E.R.A. 5th Class A. Hastings, P/MX 51755; E.R.A. 5th Class D. Blackmor, P/MX 51737; E.R.A. 5th Class E. Jacobs, P/MX 51759; E.R.A. 5th Class Robert Hayhow; Cpl. R.M. Arthur D. Ketcher, PO/K 956; Marine Brinley A. Pritchard, PO/X 2818; Marine James A. Hartley, PO/X 2157; Marine Edwin J. Fidler, PO 21789; Sy. P.O. Norman Finley, P/M 38965; S.B.A. Reginald Bendell, P/MX 56570; P.O. Steward John Perruci, L 13358 (Maltese); Steward Laurence Mallis, E/LX22995 (Maltese); James V. Hearn.

THIRD LIST

Capt. W. G. Benn; Cmdr. R. F. Nicholls.

Pay Cmdr. John R. Cundall; Sub-Lt. Douglas R. Wheeler; Mid. Ronald M. Seaburn-May; Lt. Anthony H. Terry; Surg. Lt. Dick Caldwell; Lt. Henry Duncan; Lt.-Cmdr. Frederick N. Cook, R.A.N.; Lt. (E.) Richard S. Wallace; Sub-Lt. Anthony H. Pearman, R.N.V.R.; Senior Master George Prowse; Mid. Norman W. Rockingham; Cadet Peter H. Owen; Sub-Lt. Frederick Combes, R.N.R.; Pay. Lt. Anthony P. Wilkinson; Gunner Edward A. Evans; Wt. Eng. Frank J. Bulley; Wt. Eng. Edward Whitbread; Bosn. Frank Williams; Lt. Gerald Affleck-Graves; Pay. Lt.-Cmdr. Eardley G. S. MacLean; Lt.-Cmdr. Thomas F. Wisden; Surg. Cmdr. George L. Ritchie; Lt.-Cmdr. Michael R. F. Ward; Lt.-Cmdr. Richard A. B. Gregory; Lt.-Cmdr. James P. Ingpen; Sub-Lt. Peter Richard; Lt. Claude E. L. Schlater; Pay. Lt. William E. Sandifers R.N.R.; Sub-Lt. Kenneth B. Clayton, R.N.V.R.; Sub-Lt. Jaffrey T. E. Vincent.

Sub-Lt. Daniel W. Hall; Pay. Sub-Lt. Gilbert S. Harrison, R.N.V.R.; Mid. John K. Smithalls; Pay. Cadet Michael G. H. Mawson; Sub-Lt. (E.) Wm. M. Hutchison, R.N.V.R.; Eng. Cmdr. J. W. Renshaw; Lt. Bernard B. Keen; Cmd. Gunner Benjamin J. Anslow; Lt. Michael H. Benten, R.M.; Pay. Lt.-Cmdr. Arthur F. Blowers; Sig. Bsn. James G. Warren; Act. W.S.O. Gwyn Protheroe; Pay. Lt. Harold J. C. Woods, R.N.R.; Mid. Roger P. Pirie.

E.R.A. 5th class William A. Dunne, P/MX 51749; Chief Stoker Philip Terry, P/K 5828; S.V. Boy George Trewinnard, P/JX 154953; Off. C.K.1 Paolo Spitari, P/L 11341; Off. C.K.3 Edward Sammit, P/ELX 22089; Ord. Seaman Norman Lazell, P/JX 30961; Steward Arthur Chalker, P/LX 22830; Stoker 1st class John Henry Makin, O/KX 91325; A.B. Samuel Borthwick, P/SSX 21110; A.B. John Murray, P/SSX 24002; Marines William Smith, JP/20886; John Breen, P/X 11; S.E. Barry Hawes, P/X 2329; James W. D. Shuter, P/X 3138; Henry J. Goodson, P/217063; A.B. Samuel P. Head, P/SSX 24815; Leading Cooks Frederick J. Ransome, P/MX 50641; Frederick S. Clements, P/MX 50868; Rufus Baker, P/MX 49253; Henry C. Balch, P/MX 48390; A.B. Thomas J. Foster, P/SSX 20208; L.S. John Harty, P/JX 129560; William A. Edwards, P/JX 129463; Marine Bertram H. Hilkin, P/X 3129; L.S. Alfred T. Pitcher, P/JX 125809; Seaman Edward S. Stewart, X 20405, R.N.R.; O.S. Ronald Kitchener, P/SS X 27421; A.B. Tom S. Coulson, P/SS X 21097; Boy L.C. Gordon E. Dove, P/JX 158090; O.S. William F. Sidley, P/SS X 25548; Alfred Hickmore, P/SS X 26108.

C.P.O. Cook Joseph F. Pray, P/M 36321; P.O. Albert E. Seymour, P/J 77929; O.S. William Lawrence, P/JX 158559; Boy Ronald V. Harbord, P/JX 157776; Boy Arthur Smith, P/JX 158351; L. Tel. James R. Melrose, P/J 62858; Tels. Frederick L. Hawts, P/SSX 14241; Robert C. Grove, P/JX 145852; Boy Tel. Ernest F. Upham, P/JX 156091; Sig. Kenneth J. Conway, P/JX 152680; L. Tel. Raymond S. Jones, P/JX 140264; Boy L./C. Frank McCarthy, P/JX 159894; L.S. Edward J. Harris, P/J 108343; William P. Casey, P/JX 129517; O.S. Ronald D. Burton, P/SSX 29335; Ivor H. Pagett, P/SSX 27284; A.B. Peter J. Morris, P/JX 140837; O.S. Robert M. Ward, P/SSX 27943; L.S.A. Frank C. Sims, P/MX 54629; E.R.A. George W. C. Atmeare, P/MX 55657; Marine Desmond P. O'Byrne, P/2912; O.S. George Smith, P/SSX 26094; Matthew Bowes, P/SSX 27278; Leonard Seal, P/SSX 27285.

FOURTH LIST

O.S. Allen D. Brown, P/SSX27212; Boy, 1st Class, Clarence J. Hall, P/JX157395; E.R.A., 5th Class, James T. Whitlock, P/MX600; A.B. Ellis Clarke, P/SSX19535; Boy, 1st Class, Douglas Newton, P/JX158448; Boy, 1st Class, Albert V. Frost, P/JX156558; Marine Aubrey S. Amer, P/X2746; Marine Frank White, P/X2414; Marine Alfred J. Wheatland, P/X3301; Marine Thomas R. Drew, P/X3131; Sto. Robert Lees, P/KX85979; Sto. James Burnside, P/KX86764; Sto. Cecil J. Lucking, P/KX86764; Sto. Norman Butcher, P/K61752; Sto. Edward Fleming, P/K60057; E.R.A. James A. Cuade, P/MX53744; Cpl. R. M. John J. Coombes, P/D1083; Cpl. R. M. John A. Payton, P/X1576; Marine Jack L. Halford, P/X3058; Boy Edward R. Britt, P/JX160645; Ch.E.R.A. Cyril J. Wilson, P/M35564; O.S. George P. Stephen, P/JX156701; Sgt. R. M. George E. T. Parham, P/OX237; Ldg. Cook James D. F. O'Leary, P/MX51038; Asst. Cook Thomas W. R. Taylor, P/MX58213; Ldg. Cook Leonard Bryan, P/MX51476; Cpl. R. M. George H. Woolnough, P/O22649; Marine Jack E. Bryant, P/O3046; Sto. P. O. Gordon Whitehouse, P/K65712; Sto. P. O. William G. Bourling, P/KX85051; Sto. P. O. John Wm. Welch, P/K64277; Blacksmith Arthur R. F. Gibbs, P/MX58511; Marine William Hughlock, P/OX3039; Ldg. Sto. Charles W. T. Murrin, P/KX82587; Marine Leslie H. Tunnicliffe, P/OX2352; Painter Edgar L. Scott, P/MX59247.

Ch. Shpt. Reginald W. G. Whincup, P/MX54093; Joiner Frederick W. Wiltshire, P/MX53765; C.P.O. Wtr. Stanley W. H. Thompson, P/MX45078; Marine A. Lawrence Archer, P/X1714; C.P.O. George F. Vennel, P/J93886; Walter G. Palmer, P/JX144293; Boy L/C. Donald J. Hart, P/JX157014; A.B. Arthur Brierley, P/JX141034; A.B. Herbert Wright, P/JX146523; Marine Michael F. Davey, P/OX2283; Musn. George B. Williams, RMB/X188; Boy, 1st Cl., Frank O'N. Dall, P/JX158264; Boy, 1st Cl., Ronald C. Green, P/JX159260; A.G. Roger Ashley, P/JX106833.

FIFTH LIST

Marine Kenneth J. J. Wood, P/XX 2940; L.S. Henry G. Symonds, P/J 98970; A.B. Alfred H. Bevis, P/J 94370; Ldg. Sto. George A. Langlands, P/KX 77751; Sto. 2nd Class Douglas W. V. Sheldrick, P/KX 95686; Sto. 2nd Class Robert H. Bateman, P/KX 95685; Ldg. Sto. Kenneth Hickman, P/KX 75044; Sto. Eric E. Lidget, P/KX 85116; A.B. Arthur Gearing, P/J 50173; Sto. Reginald Morley, P/KX 86242; Boy Reuben W. Askham, P/JX 157881; L.S. Fred Cross, P/SSX 15358; O.S. Herbert H. Potts, P/SSX 27549; Marine Ronald Joran, P/X 2166; Marine Frederick Hanharan, P/X 668; L. Sig. William J. Forsey, P/J 115093; Sto. P.O. William A. Cripps, P/K 63361; Off. Steward Paulo Zarb, E/LX 22994; Boy 1st Class George R. White, P/JX 157516; Marine Thomas W. Potter, P/X 3034; O.S. Stanley Cole, P/SSX 27850; Boy Tel. Kenneth Harrington, P/JX 156417; A.B. William H. Smart, P/JX 125270; Boy 1/c Arthur W. Smith, P/JX 158676; A.B. John Farquahar, P/SSX 20205; A.B. Sydney Evans, P/SSX 19545; A.B. John E. Hasler, P/SSX 20749; L.S.A. William G. Betterbury, P/MX 55409; L. Wtr. Kenneth H. Willoughby, P/MX 51080; L. Wtr. Leonard Childs, P/MX 52088.

A.B. Ernest E. Davies, P/J 114121; A.B. Henry W. Pither, PJX 139319; Marine Frederick A. Martin, PO/X 2032; Boy Henry P. T. Cox, P/JX 158669; Boy Albert R. Turney, P/JX 158967; Boy Gordon F. Cook, P/JX 157925; O.S. John T. Lettin, P/SSX 27219; Boy Reginald P. Watten, P/JX 158402; Boy Arthur Allridge, P/JX 158666; Cpl. R. M. Norman T. Davies, P/X 523; A.B. Edward C. Alford, P/J 104258; Cpl. R. M. Herbert Pattison, P/X 720; E.R.A. Ronald Connor, P/MX 51745; Boy Victor R. Thompson, P/JX 155604; O.S. Kenneth E. Davidson, P/SSX 29658; A.B. Percy Neville P/JX 133076; A.B. George A. Smith, P/J 108735; Marine Arthur G. Coote, PO/X 3130; Ch. Sto. Alfred Lawrence, P/K 61871; Ch. Sto. Frederick J. Hobbs, P/K 56827; Mech. William H. Throssel, P/K 62436; A.B. James E. Hollis, P/JX 127535; Ch. E.R.A. Charles P. Cartwright, P/M 22632; A.B. George F. Baker, P/J 89966.

Capt. W. G. Benn, who is among the survivors, took command of the Royal Oak last July. He had previously commanded the aircraft carrier Argus. From 1935 to 1938 he was Director of Navigation at the Admiralty.

SIXTH LIST

A.B. (RFR) Frank Cutler, P/J 82017; Ord. Tel. James Charles Devlin, P/SSX 25285; P.O. Teleg. Thomas H. Lakin, P/JS 131350; E.A. 4th Class Ronald Hall, P/MX 56010; Musn. Charles S. Bignell, PMB; Marine Albert E. Tuttom, P/X 21442; A.B. Alfred J. Farley, P/J; L.S. David J. Lloyd, P/JX 127371; L.S. Reginald C. Green, P/J 114777; L.S. Reginald H. Finlayson, P/J 113307; A.B. Mac Williams, P/JX 129358; L.S. Allen J. Babb, P/J 114593; L.S. George R. Poling, P/JX 139331; A.B. Henry Pipes, P/SSX 19750; Yeo. Sigs. Ronald S. Howell, D/JX 129115; R.P.O. John H. Smith, P/M 40125; A.B. William E. Woodnutt, P/J 101342; S.B.C.P.O. Clifford Westcott, P/M 36264; Ord. Smn. George L. J. Lockyer, P/SSX 27291; S.B.C.P.O. Henry W. Main, P/MX 45033; Ldg. Sto. John Coady, P/KX 77056; Boy Ronald E. Wilson, P/JX 158406; Musn. Alfred L. Fordham, RMB 534; Act. Cpl. R.M. George R. Andrews, CH 23245; A.B. Kenneth B. Forder, P/J 98874; Marine Arthur J. Moppett, PO/X 190; Marine William Owens, PO/X 519; A.B. R.N.R. James Ross, PX 10049 B.

Sea. R.N.R. Thomas Merrick, PX 21125 A; Boy William Weir, P/JX 139132; A.B. (R.F.R.) Wilfred Nichols, P/J 101486; Boy John Hall, P/JX 158228; Boy Herbert E. Pocock, P/JX 158225; Boy Stanley W. Haigh, P/JX 158966; O.S. Charles H. Riley, P/SSX 27287; O.S. (1.C.) Anthony Camenzul, Malta/LX 20813; L.S. George J. Maggs, P/JX 127943; L.S. Alfred J. Hoskin, P/J 84934; P.O. George J. Childs, P/JX 132128; P.O. (Pens.) Arthur W. Scarff, P/255898; Sto. 1st-class Reginald A. Pope, P/K 67304; Act. L.S. James D. Haig, P/JX 139932; Ldg. Sto. John W. J. Clayton, P/KX 77431; Ldg. Sea James A. Radford, P/JX 134281; Act. P.O. Victor Cruse, P/JX 143568; Marine Alexander R. Howard, PO 22278; P.O. Ernest J. Gilmore, P/J 106443; Boy John P. Billingham, P/JX 158467; O.S. Lawrence W. Millican, P/SSX 27562; A.B. George R. Arnell, P/J 96094; A.B. Victor L. T. Ayles, P/SSX 18356; P.O. Thomas B. Stevens, P/JX 131787; A.B. Walter Thomas Weare, P/J 107185; Sto. (1/C.) John Brown, P/KX 85193; Sto. (1/C.) Albert Bond, P/KX 84270; Musn. (R.M.) John F. P. Thomson, School of Music, Deal, XL 1076.

C.P.O. OK William E. Hunnby, P/MX 45002; Boy (1/c) Stanley R. Wood, P/JX 156601; Sto. (1/C) William M. Campbell, P/KX 91407; Act. P.O. William J. Barsdell, P/JX 125808; Marine Edward A. Moore, P/20711; P.O. Tel. Thomas A. Noble, P/J 111162; Ldg. Sto. Thomas H. Jones, P/KX 76174; Marine Norman J. Hine, P/X 3044; O.S. Donald T. Harris, P/SSX 26429; Marine Stanley Rowlands, P/X 2005; Boy Kenneth H. Took, P/JX 160118; O.S. Dennis W. Masters, P/SSX 27558; O.S. Eric D. Densham, P/SSX 27214; O.S. Philip A. White, P/SSX 27554; Boy (1/C) Matthew Skilling, P/JX 157809; O.S. Richard H. Gardiner, P/SSX 27542; Boy (1/C) Cyril G. Lipscombe, VP/JX 157750; O.S. Thomas G. Bishop, P/JX 3537; A.B. Ronald J. Kenny, P/SSX 17055; Joiner Edward Randall, P/MX 59551; Musn. Cyril S. Poultney, RMB/X 564; Marine Richard H. Wood, PO/X 2911; Boy (1 C) John N. Mead, P/JX 56201; A.B. Frederick M. Gattrell, PJ/10793; Musn. R.M.B. Horace A. G. Kelly, RMB X9; E.R.A. Edwin H. Fairner, P/MX 51513; Ldg. Sto. George E. Winterbottom, P/KX 78699; Ldg. Sto. Henry J. Lutman, P/KX 81472; O.H. E.R.A. Norman V. Pead, P/M 35031; Cpl. R.M. James McLaverty, P/02208; Marine Norman W. Grant, P/X 2949; P.O. (O.K.) James Chalder, P/M 39079; R.P.O. Walter G. Phillips, P/M 40186; Chf. Sto. William H. Aplin, P/K 56312; E.R.A. 4th Class Robert Edmunds, P/MX 49501; Sgt. R.M. George H. Booth, P/A X 421; Marine Frank Brooke, P/X 2815; A.B. (Pens.) Henry Bryant, P/J 21247; Marine Gerald Ellis, P/X 3051; A.B. Sidney R. Dawson, P/JX 152539; L.S. Jesse Sherwood, P/J 114143; Act. P.O. Thomas W. A. Blundell, P/JX 135774; L.S. (R.N.R.) John R. Goodland, P/X 10451.

A.B. Joseph Figg, P/JX 145559; O.S. Norman L. Hinde, P/SSX 27406; L.S. Harry Farmer, P/JX 128802; O.C.1. Williams E. Chown, D/LX 20100; P.C. Std. Alfred G. Ines, D/L 14837; Sig. William K. Hutchings, D/JX 144680; E.R.A. 3rd class William A. Marsh, P/MX 54600; Ch. Mech. (Pen.) Jack Timmis, P/K 21465; Ch. Mech. (Pen.) Robert L. Adams, P/K 42003; Ch. Mech. Thomas F. Freer, P/K 63476; Marine Richard H. Orges, PO/X 2753; Marine Norman E. Thackeray, PO/X 2598; Marine Ronald S. Miles, PO/X 3074; Marine Alex G. Chatfield, PO/X 1821; A.B. David H. Ward, P/J 89997; Sto. William Couch, P/KX 87728; L.S. Edward A. Boxall, P/JX 131858; Sto. Harry V. Dowling, P/KX 89504; Sto. Thomas Harland, P/KX 93912; Sto. Herbert R. Johnston, P/RX 90179; Musn. (Deal) Fernleigh G. Judge, RMB X 640; C.P.O. Kenneth G. Dewey, P/J 107188; A.B. Jim Collier, P/J 76728; Musn. (Deal) Harold J. Wernham, RMB X 681 (Deal); Musn. Philip C. W. Combes, RHB X 747; Musn. Dennis S. Cook, RMB X 543; (S.B.) P.O. William S. Brieden, P/M 39261; Marine Reginald A. Turner, PO 22167; Marine Stanley R. Saltmarsh, PO/X 2285.

SEVENTH LIST

Lt. K. R. S. Leadley, R.N.; Midshipman P. D. Sturdee, R.N.

Reginald G. Sylvester, Pensioner P.O. J 4383; Walter Barrett, Sto. P.O., PK 59292; Ronald Frank Stimson, Sto. 1.C., PKX 84323; Edward Harris, E.R.A., 5th Class, PMX 59081; Alfred Redman, R.N.R., A.B., 7203; John Alter, Ldg. Seaman, PJX 143115; Norman Claude Robertson, Tel., DJX 152302; Ian Bell, O. Sig., PJX 147378; Reginald George Birch, Ord. Sea., PSSX 29655; Andrew Paterson, Sto. C., PKX 86701; Maurice Blake, A.B., PSSX 16166; Wilfred Gibson, Chief E.R.A., PMX 32893; George William Fisher, A.B., PX 147635; Michael Connelly, Sto., 1st Class, PKX 87556; Arthur H. Knott, A.B., P/J 99993; Robert E. Jackson, Ord. Tel., P/JX 157197.

EIGHTH LIST

C.P.O. Mech. H. Bish, P.O. C. W. Ball, L.S. R. Tilley, E.R.A. W. H. Crowther, E.R.A. T. R. Storar, Sto. P. Rose, Sto. H. F. Wadham, A.B. R. Anderson, A.B. H. J. Woods, A.B. H. S. Le-Poidevin, Sto. H. Howe, Tel. W. H. Clark, A.B. L. H. Roberts, Sig. J. H. Lee.

Sub-Lt. Kersley, R.N.R.; Mid. W. T. J. Fox, Mid. M. F. J. Symes-Thompson.

Sto. P.O. Sydney Henry Cook.

Reproduced by kind permission of The Daily Telegraph.

Günther Prien was born in Osterfeld, Germany, on the 16th January, 1908. He became a sailor at the age of fifteen and by 1923 he was an officer in the Hamburg Amerika Line.

In 1933 Prien joined the German Navy. In 1938 he was given command of U-47. Two years after sinking HMS Royal Oak Prien was credited with destroying 28 merchant ships. While leading a wolfpack attack on an Allied convoy, he was killed when the U-47 was sunk on the 6th March, 1941.

Kapitän-leutnant Günther Prien

***U-47* entering Krupps dockyards**

Prien's Mad Bull insignia on the conning tower. His insignia was adopted by the 7th U-flotilla.

Courtesy of Mark Bentley, Tiger Collectibles, 2004.

The crew of *U-47* were given a welcome in

at the airport in Berlin after sinking the *Royal Oak*

Crowds gathered in the streets of Berlin to welcome the crew of the *U-47* after she returned from sinking the *Royal Oak*

Thousands of people lined the route of the victory parade held in honour of the crew of the *U-47* when she returned to Germany after sinking the *Royal Oak*

Hitler congratulates Kapitän-leutnant Günther Prien

Günther Prien was awarded the Knight's Cross, Germany's highest honour, and the whole crew took lunch with Hitler.

Prien and the crew of the *U-47* dine with Hitler

An artist's impression of the wreck of *HMS Royal Oak*. The deck now lies at approximately 45 degrees to the sea bed and most of the superstructure is crushed beneath the upturned hull.

The *Royal Oak*'s 50-feet steam pinnace went down with the battleship to the sea bed as the *Royal Oak* rolled over on top of her.

She now lies crushed beneath the wreck.

Land was only 1000 yards away but few survivors reached its safety. The plaque on the original marker buoy reads 'This marks the wreck of *HMS Royal Oak* and the grave of her crew. Respect their resting place. Unauthorised diving prohibited.'

Reproduced with kind permission of Charles Tait, St. Ola, Orkney

The modern buoy that now marks the *Royal Oak's* final resting place

March 8th 1941

U-47, commanded by one of Germany's greatest submarine commanders, Günther Prien, is sunk by the British destroyer, *Wolverine*, when she attacks convoy OB293.

Günther Prien went aboard for his last patrol on the 20th February 1941

Memories of HMS Royal Oak

The following is taken from the account (published in the Orcadian, October 18th 2001) of an ordinary seaman (Able Seaman Stanley Ivan Cole) who, at the age of 18, survived the sinking of HMS *Royal Oak* in Scapa Flow on the 14th October 1939. He is now believed to be deceased.

During the day and evening of the 13th October, the men were kept busy taking on and stowing stores. Able Seaman Stanley Cole and a close mess-mate, Bill, from the Newcastle-on-Tyne area, turned in at about 21.00 hours. The last sounds to be heard were the duty working parties going through the mess-decks closing down the heavy hatches and watertight doors.

The first explosion woke all on the mess-deck and they swung out of their hammocks to see what it was all about. The story was that it was either a carbon monoxide bottle exploding or something in the paint store – right forward. Some even said the anchor cable had snapped because of the rapidly deteriorating weather conditions. His mate Bill said "I don't like this, I'm going up top", and off he went; he never saw him again. Believing the situation to be not serious, many turned-in again, but, about 10 minutes later, he heard two very loud explosions, separated by only seconds, and the ship began to list and the lighting failed. Secondary lights working off batteries did not seem to be very effective, and there began a crush of men making for the ladder to the next deck up. He had pulled on his overall suit over his underpants and attempted to grab his plimsolls but they slid down the sloping mess-deck, out of sight. There was a lot of milling and jostling at the foot of the ladder, and he was aware of a lighter being struck and a voice of authority calling for no panic. By the feeble light, he could just make out a face and a Chief Petty Officer's cap. His abandon-ship station was to report to the port-side whaler – one of the battleship's boats. He was one of the crew of five men on the oars, in charge of a coxswain, usually a leading seaman.

The boat deck was several decks up. Stanley, still not thinking the ship would sink although it was listing considerably, struggled to get through to the ladders; he was concerned about the consequences of not being at his place of duty. Finally, gaining his objective, still in darkness, he soon established that he was the only one there and wondered why he had heard no orders or instruction over the ship's tannoy. The whaler weighed about a ton and a half and, due to the list, was pressed hard against the davits. He had to support himself by clinging to the guard-rails. Having no knife, he could not even cut through the ropes for hoisting, or lowering, and it occurred to him that even if he had been able to, the boat could have crashed down the ship's side and sustained damage. It might even have crashed down on to some of the swimmers already in the water.

He decided it was time to go, although he still did not think the ship would sink. He pulled himself through the lower gap of the guard-rail and launched himself in a half dive, half slithering movement down the ship's side. He got so far down before his right foot became jammed in the guttering of the 'blister' (the anti-torpedo bulge, which seemed not to have been effective on the starboard side). He stayed trapped, head down, for several seconds until he was able to free himself by pushing with his hands before slipping on down into the water. He could smell the oil fuel and could not avoid getting some in his mouth, nose and ears, but he kept his eyes closed until he surfaced. Coughing and spluttering he became aware that his right foot and leg seemed to be hanging in the water as he began to swim away from the ship's side, along with some others.

It was like trying to swim through liquid tar, and he was convinced he wasn't going to make it. The water was bitterly cold and, from all around him in the darkness, he could hear cries for help from injured, burned, despairing bodies. Kicking out as best he could with his good leg, he was sure he could feel bodies of drowned ship-mates under his foot. His hand caught something – a small piece of wood about 2 feet long by 6 inches wide – and he hung on to it in the blind faith that it would keep him afloat! He would probably have killed anyone who tried to take it from him! Then, another stroke of luck – what he took to be a five-gallon oil drum came within range and he tried to hold his arm over it as it slipped and rolled in the oil.

Finally, after what seemed like ages, he made out three or four bobbing heads paddling slowly along with a length of timber that he supposed could have been one of the 'deals' they had adapted for seating for the church services. He let go of the drum, but not his small scrap of wood, and joined up with the lads paddling the deal. They tried shouting and singing with hoarse throats without success, growing ever colder and more exhausted. One of their number slipped off the plank and they never saw him again.

His last view of the battleship *Royal Oak* was of her keel, silhouetted against the dark sky-line. She appeared to have turned right over. Then, just as he had all but given up the struggle, along came a ship's whaler, and he felt himself being hauled over the boat's side and dumped, with two or three other lads on top of him, in a cold, sodden, oily heap. On the drifter *Daisy II*, skipper John Gatt and his crew, were valiantly dragging scores of bodies from the water, until *Daisy* herself was in danger of capsizing under the sheer weight of numbers. The *Daisy* transferred them to the sea-plane carrier *Pegasus* whose crew did whatever they could for them: washing them down with hot, clean water and turning out their lockers for every item of spare clothing and anything else they could get hold of.

Stanley was treated by the sick-bay staff, who dressed his foot in wads of cotton wool and wooden splints, gave him shots of pain-killer, then lifted him into someone's vacated hammock. They opened their canteen to give the survivors whatever there was to be had – cigarettes, chocolate, biscuits – anything. The following morning they were transferred to the armed liner *Voltaire*, then on to the hospital ship *Abba*. His foot and leg had sustained fractures and was encased in plaster of Paris.

Another harrowing story was how the boy seamen's mess-deck became a mass of flame from the burning cordite. Many of the boys, aged around 15, had joined the *Royal Oak* about three weeks before, from a shore training establishment. An able seaman was said to have gone back to the boy's mess-deck to help some of them to escape, only to lose his own life. One has to pay tribute to *Daisy II* and Skipper Gatt and his men, without whom many more would have died in one of the worst tragedies in British naval history.

Able Seaman Stanley Ivan Cole
Orkney Library Photographic Archives

David Turner

HMS Royal Oak – A Boy's Story

Men swam in sea of oil

It was revealed by Mr Churchill in the House of Commons, yesterday, Wednesday October 13th 1939, that the full story of the end of *Royal Oak*, sunk at anchor by the most daring U-boat feat of the war, was told last night by a boy survivor, 18-year-old Vincent Marchant of Doncaster.

Marchant was asleep in his hammock when the first explosion rocked the ship. He ran to the upper deck to see what had happened. Twenty minutes later, there was a second explosion, followed by a third – then a fourth. By that time, the ship was listing and sinking rapidly. He remembered what had happened in the *Courageous*, his previous ship. So he stripped himself of all his clothing and, tying his safety belt around his waist, dived into the water.

Hundreds of heads

Searchlights, playing over the surface of the water, picked out hundreds of heads bobbing around in the water. Great volumes of oil started to belch up to the surface. His eyes started to smart, and the faces of all the men swimming in the water turned a greasy black. He was caught in a searchlight for several minutes and saw that two of his pals were swimming alongside him. Later, however, they got cramp and went under for the last time.

Marchant, now in hospital, swam and swam in the sea of oil; he didn't know for how long but said that he must have gone about a mile and a half when he felt a rock under him. He scarcely remembered what happened after that. It was like a nightmare. He was dazed and half-conscious and just had a vague recollection of climbing up the sheer face of a cliff about 20 to 30ft high to safety. Some time later – he would say about half an hour – six men arrived with restoratives. They wrapped him in a blanket and took him to an hotel in the town nearby.

Four victims of the sinking of the battleship *Royal Oak*, were buried at sea yesterday, October 17th 1939. Their bodies had been landed at Kirkwall.

These articles, first published on 18th October, 1939, are adapted with the kind permission of the Daily Mail.

Many boy seamen were killed when the *Royal Oak* was sunk

The caption reads: 'For three generations the Priestlys, a Portsmouth family, have had men serving in the Royal Marines. Fifteen-years-old John (above) followed in their footsteps. He became a drummer boy... died in the *Royal Oak*'

"Drifters men" of Britain's Royal Navy

The entire transport of personnel, of food supply and of mail to British warships at anchor is carried out by drifters, which in peacetime were simple fishing boats. Manned by their hardy fishermen crews, these small craft now act in all weathers as ferries, water carriers, target-towing vessels and as hospital boats to the Royal Navy. Many of the drifter men have received decorations for bravery, including the Victoria Cross.

Another well known drifter skipper is 40 year old John Gatt, DSC, from Rosehearty on the North-East coast of Scotland. He won his DSC at the beginning of the war for rescuing 386 survivors from the torpedoed battleship (*Royal Oak*). He treasures even more than his DSC a silver watch presented to him by the parents and friends of the men he saved.

Admiralty 16/09/1941

A special dedication to the late crew of the *Daisy II* who wished their story to be told

Johnnie Duthie, a crew member, never thought that he would be in the company of men with so much courage in the face of peril on the sea. They all had great faith and that is what kept them going; their strength that night was beyond human endurance. They gave their all, and asked for nothing. They all worked together that night as a team, picking men out of the water, their strength ebbing all the time.

The Skipper, John Gatt DSC, never lost his great courage all through that night in October, 1939, but, as the long dawn came, there was a deadly silence in Scapa Flow, because over 800 men were still missing and no longer had any chance of survival. By the time dawn broke, they were now just six men, confused and tired, but, amidst the sorrow that so many brave sailors had lost their lives, they had the joy of knowing that they had rescued 360 men from a watery grave.

Luckily for the drifter, *Daisy II*, and her crew, they had moored alongside the port side of the *Royal Oak* and were thus clear of the initial devastating explosions. Johnnie Duthie recalled that they had gone to bed, only to be awakened by a massive explosion. They went up on deck and a Naval Officer from the battleship asked what was happening. Nobody seemed to know, but there was some speculation that the explosion had been made by a bomb dropped from a German aircraft which had escaped before the shore batteries could open fire.

For some reason, Johnnie Duthie didn't go back to bed, although the other members of the crew did. But they were to get little sleep, for there was another tremendous explosion around six to eight minutes after the first one. After the second explosion, they stood with their skipper on the deck and watched the great battleship roll over within six minutes of being torpedoed and all around them men were crying for help.

At that point, they had to fight to save their own boat as the mighty battleship began to keel over lifting the drifter by her mooring ropes out of the sea. The *Daisy II* was held by ropes from stern and bow to the battleship's port side. The drifter was in imminent danger of going under. When the crew saw what was happening, they ran forward and cut the rope at the stern and immediately the *Daisy II* dropped away from the side [illegible] rapidly submerging battleship.

There were so many acts of bravery that night and it was just something that was done because it had to be done. There was no time to think, everything happened so quickly and with little or no warning, leaving everyone in a state of shock.

Regardless of their own safety, the entire crew of the *Daisy II* began to pluck their unfortunate comrades from this turbulent, frothing pit of hell. The task of picking survivors out of the dark, murky water became increasingly more difficult. Escaping furnace oil from the battleship was pouring into the sea and, as the twisted metal hurtled downwards to the ocean bed, the crude black mass floated continually upwards, flooding the surface with a thick greasy film, and creating havoc among the struggling survivors. After the final flame was swallowed up and the sea engulfed the last lingering piece of wreckage, the night sky plunged Scapa Flow into a deathly darkness.

Daisy II was amidst hundreds of sailors shouting for help and deliverance from their plight. Hauling the sailors up on to the gas-lit drifter became a soul-destroying job – for all were a pitiful sight. Many were wounded and badly burned. One sailor called out to them and said that he could not see as oil was in his eyes. Although they tried to get hold of him, he kept swimming further into the darkness still crying for help. Another rescued sailor with pluck and determination insisted that he re-enter the murky depths again and again to pull his shipmates clear of the deadly furnace oil. A doctor serving on board HMS *Royal Oak* was lifted onto the drifter and he tirelessly treated his injured patients.

The strain must have been hard on the rescuers surrounded by such afflictions and the last call of those who were giving up the fight became a chilling experience. Like the sailor who, with his last breath, uttered "Say goodbye to my wife and children". That is why I am sure none of the crew of the Daisy II ever forgot the experiences they went through that night. It was a horrendous experience for all involved; the mental, as well as the physical torture was to last a lifetime.

John Gatt, the Skipper, remained calm throughout, giving orders in a quiet, controlled voice and maneuvering the drifter easily amongst the battleship's survivors, aiding the crew to bring the drowning sailors on board. The last survivors they took aboard were a terrible sight for them all. Their skin hung in shreds down their arms, they all had a lost look in their eyes and sometimes when they were being hauled on to the drifter they often shouted "Don't touch me".

Without *Daisy II*, her skipper John Gatt and his crew, many more would have died in one of the worst tragedies in British Naval History.

Their courage must never be forgotten

Daisy II

The Crew of *Daisy II*

John Gatt, DSC, from Rosehearty, skipper of the *Daisy II*.

John Stephen

John Gardener

Johnnie Duthie

[illegible]

Robbie Duthie

The simple wooden crosses used immediately after the funerals were later replaced by granite crosses

My Pilgrimage to the *Royal Oak*

In September 2003, I finally honoured my schoolboy promise to visit my uncle's war grave, and make the moving trip to a site of sorrow, where 26 of the dead lie.

I laid a wreath and with it a laminated message, from me, my Mother, her younger brother, and other relatives, which said:

"You are still sadly missed."

When I walked into the cemetery, the sun was shining from a clear blue sky, the air was still, there was nothing to disturb the peace and tranquillity of the moment. It was an emotional experience I will never forget.

I also went to visit the site of the *Royal Oak* itself and scattered flowers on the sea in memory of all those men who went down with the ship. I felt a sense of great sadness for all those whose lives had been lost. That same evening, as the sun was setting over Scapa Flow, I flew low over the wreck site in a light aircraft, and on to the Churchill barriers.

I returned to Manchester on the 11th September 2003 after four unforgettable days at Scapa Flow. I related my experience to my Mother who is now 93, she was delighted that, after all these years, a member of the family had finally made the journey to her elder brother's last resting place.

Commander Woodrow-Clark was just 33 when he was killed. He left a wife who is now deceased, and a son, Michael, from whom the family have not heard for a number of years but who I hope will make contact.

My promise, made to my mother 64 years ago, and my personal ambition have been accomplished.

I approach the Royal Navy Cemetery on Hoy to place a tribute to my late uncle. Note the permanent granite crosses

At the site of the sinking of the mighty battleship HMS *Royal Oak*

David Turner

Lyness Naval Cemetery

Here rest the heroes from some of the most famous incidents in modern naval history – the Battle of Jutland (1916); *HMS Hampshire* sunk by a mine off Bursary (1916); explosion of the *Vanguard* off Flotta (1917); and the *Royal Oak* torpedoed in Scapa Flow.

At the end of the First World War, the German High Seas Fleet was interned at Scapa Flow in Orkney, pending Armistice negotiations. On 21st June 1919, Admiral von Reuter gave the command for seventy-four German battleships, cruisers and destroyers to be scuttled rather than fall into British hands.

**HMS *Royal Oak* funeral, October 16th, 1939.
Procession to cemetery, Lyness**

**HMS *Royal Oak* funeral, October 16th, 1939.
Procession to cemetery, Lyness, including survivors dressed in overalls**

HMS *Royal Oak* funeral, October 16th, 1939.
Procession to cemetery, Lyness

HMS *Royal Oak* funeral, October 16th, 1939.
Procession to cemetery, Lyness

HMS *Royal Oak* funeral, October 16th, 1939.
At the graveside, Lyness Naval Cemetery

Memorial plaque, St Magnus Cathedral, Kirkwall, Orkney
Reproduced with kind permission of Charles Tait, St. Ola, Orkney

A memorial plaque to the men of the *Royal Oak* was erected in St Magnus Cathedral, Kirkwall, together with the ship's bell, recovered from the sea bed of Scapa Flow. The plaque was unveiled on the 14th October, 1948, the ninth anniversary of the tragedy, by Rear Admiral W.G. Benn, who was Captain of the warship on the night she sank, at a service attended by several other survivors of that terrible event of war in 1939. Each day in the Cathedral, one page of a Book of Condolence is turned in memory of the 833 officers and men who lost their lives.

The unfurling of a battle ensign on the upturned hull of the battleship *Royal Oak* by a Royal Navy diver on the anniversary of her sinking

Former enemies united by the same tragedy: *Royal Oak* sailor, Welshman Taffy Davies and Herbert Herman, crewman on the *U-47*, meet at a reunion in Portsmouth

David Turner

Reducing The Threat To Wildlife In Scapa Flow

For over 60 years, HMS *Royal Oak* has lain undisturbed, a grave for the 833 men who died when the battleship was torpedoed by a U-boat.

The fight to preserve the dignity of the wreck in Scapa Flow, off Orkney, has grown fiercer in recent years as the thousands of tonnes of oil seeping from the corroding hull threaten environmental disaster and death to Scapa Flow's large seal population and several species of rare birds. The natural action of the tide and winds is pushing the oil to the surface. Divers return to the wreck of the *Royal Oak* on a regular basis to check on oil still leaking from the battleship. To date, they believe there may be 1500 tonnes of fuel remaining trapped in the upturned ship, less than half the amount that was thought to have been in the ship's tanks when she sank.

Most recent efforts by divers working for The Ministry of Defence have involved 'hot tapping' the fuel tanks to drain the oil, but the process is slow. In the past three years, the 'tapping' has drawn 670 tonnes of oil from the ship. It is thought fuel seeps from inner tanks to the outer ones, from where it can be 'drawn off' without damaging the hull or harming its status as a National War Grave.

HMS Royal Oak

HMS Royal Oak

***HMS Royal Oak* fires her massive guns**

***HMS Royal Oak* crew portrait**

HMS Royal Oak **crew photographed under her guns**

The Royal Oak in Pentland Firth

David Turner

The Spy Who Never Was?

The question remains unanswered to this day.

When visiting the Orkneys in September 2003, I was absolutely astounded to learn, from an Orcadian who wished to remain anonymous, a story concerning espionage in relation to the sinking of the battleship *HMS Royal Oak.* It is only now that I have decided to relate this story written in this book *The Ultimate Sacrifice*.

The Admiralty, deeply embarrassed and humiliated by the sinking of the *Royal Oak* in its own anchorage in Scapa Flow, assumed that *U-47* had been guided to its target by a spy in the Orkneys. MI5, the British counter-intelligence service, was promptly blamed by the Admiralty for failing to flush out the Nazi spy. MI5 agents descended *en masse* to the Orkneys in an attempt to find the elusive spy who had made this German exploit possible. The search failed.

I am indebted to Curt Reiss, an American journalist and espionage scholar for the following astounding report.

In the Spring of 1942, the *Saturday Evening Post* published an article identifying the Scapa Flow Spy as a former officer of the German Imperial Navy, Kapitän Alfred Wehring. According to the *Post* account, Wehring had been recruited in 1928 by German intelligence to be its man at Scapa Flow, which, it was believed, would be a crucial location in any coming war against the British. Wehring adopted the fictitious name of Albert Oertal, posed as a Swiss watchmaker and opened a small shop in the town of Kirkwall in the Orkneys.

Twelve years later, Wehring emerged from deep undercover and signalled to Kapitän Karl Dönitz of the U-boat Command detailed intelligence about Scapa Flow's defences, it's unpredictable currents and its navigation obstacles.

Wehring is reported to have boarded the *U-47* at the mouth of Scapa Flow, acted as a Pilot-Navigator, then returned to Germany in triumph after twelve years of deep undercover intelligence work in Scotland and the Orkneys.

After the war, Major General Vernon Q.W. Kell, then head of MI-5, wrote that "The Germans had been supplied with up to date information by a spy." In England, with peace coming nearly six years after the *Royal Oak* had been sunk, controversy continued to swirl around the event. The Admiralty it seems still clings to the strong contention that Wehring (Oertal) had been the culprit.

British journalists probing into the affair, descended on the Orkneys and failed to locate anyone who had ever known of, much less seen Alfred Wehring, who for twelve years was said to have been masquerading in Kirkwall as Albert Oertal, a Swiss watchmaker. Kapitän-leutnant Günther Prien is probably the one man who could have provided precise information.

So the question remains. Had there really been a Nazi undercover spy long embedded in the fabric of life in the Orkneys? A German who performed one of history's boldest espionage feats? Or was it only The Spy who Never Was?

David Turner

The Bismarck

On May 20th 1941, the *Bismarck*, whose size, power and awe-inspiring name made her the most feared of all German battleships left the Baltic for the Atlantic to prey on British convoys. On May 24th, it was intercepted by the battleship *HMS Prince of Wales* and the battle-cruiser *HMS Hood*, the German battleship concentrated its fire on the *Hood*, which blew up after a salvo of shells detonated her ammunition magazines. Only three of the *Hood's* 1,418 man crew survived. The *Prince of Wales* scored several hits but was damaged. Several other Royal Naval ships were deployed to shadow and to sink the *Bismarck*, including *King George V* and *Rodney* who were coming down from the North.

The Bismarck

The Commander-in-Chief (C-in-C) of the home fleet in the *King George V* signalled to all ships involved in the engagement saying 'Intend to engage the enemy at dawn from the westward with the *Rodney*'.

The sun rose at 07:15, but the light and visibility were very poor due to constant rain squalls and low clouds, and it was not until 08:30 that the C-in-C decided conditions were good enough, the *King George V* opened fire, then the *Rodney*, with answering fire from the *Bismarck*. Having been hit by torpedo from the destroyer *Cossack*, *Bismarck*'s forecastle was on fire and her speed reduced to seven or eight knots. The *Dorsetshire* was ordered to sink her with torpedoes. Thus, ended a very gallant *Bismarck* and a brave ship's company. They had fought until there was not a gun in action and their ship nothing but a battered hulk.

The battleships *King George V*, The *Prince of Wales*, the battle-cruisers *HMS Hood*, and *HMS Sheffield*, aircraft carriers *Ark Royal* and *Renown* and several destroyers including the *Cossack*, *Maori* and *Zulu*, all played a part in this, one of the biggest sea battles of World War II, leading to the German battleship's eventual destruction. Only 116 of the *Bismarck*'s crew of 2,200 survived the battle.

A huge spurt of blue flame and a gigantic column of spray alongside the *Bismarck*'s stern. This was the beginning of the end; the *Bismarck* had received a direct hit

Bismarck survivors being rescued by a Royal Navy ship

The beautiful but ill-fated *Hood*, intended to be a 31-knot version of the *Queen Elizabeth*, she remained the largest capital ship in the world until her loss

***HMS Hood*, a battlecruiser built in 1918, at anchor at Scapa Flow in 1940**

***HMS Nelson* firing her starboard 6-inch secondary guns in 1940**

HMS Renown **seen in 1940 after complete reconstruction. She carried an external degaussing cable for protection against magnetic mines**

***HMS Warspite*, the flagship of the Mediterranean fleet and the most famous battleship of World War II, with a seven-destroyer escort it sunk eight German destroyers in the second 'Battle of Narvik'. April 13th, 1940**

November 25th, 1941

The *U-331* hit the *Barham* amidships with three torpedoes from such close range that the submarine was blown to the surface. The *Barham* exploded with a loss of 862 lives.

***HMS Barham* in Gibraltar in September 1940. She had received only a superficial modernisation and new machinery between the wars**

The End of Force Z

On December 10th 1941, the Force Z South China Sea battleship, *Prince of Wales*, and the battle-cruiser *Repulse*, escorted by the destroyers *Express*, *Electra* and *Vampire*, were spotted by the Japanese submarine *I-65*, while racing to meet the Japanese invasion fleet at Kuantan, Malaya. Aircraft scouts from the cruisers *Kinu* and *Kumano* reported that the fleet had no air cover. Ninety-five aircraft from the 22nd air flotilla took off from Saigon.

They found first the destroyer Tenedos, but she escaped their bombs and proceeded. In the main attack on Force Z, two aerial torpedoes crippled the screws and rudder of the *Prince of Wales*; the *Repulse*, although damaged, managed to avoid seventeen torpedoes before being struck by eight more. Direct hits with three torpedoes and nine bombs were made on the *Prince of Wales*. Both ships were doomed. The destroyers rescued 1,924 men, and took them to Singapore.

The end of Force Z marked the end of the era of the battleship. No new battleships have since been ordered by any navy.

March 12-29th 1941

The British Mediterranean fleet led by the battleships *Barham*, *Valiant* and *Warspite* fought the 'Battle of Matapan' at night and sank three Italian cruisers and three destroyers.

December 19th 1941

As if to underline the vulnerability of the battleship, two Italian 'human torpedoes' breached the harbour defences at Alexandria and badly damaged the British battleships *Queen Elizabeth* and *Valiant* with limpet mines.

December 26th 1943

The sinking of the *Scharnhorst* while it was trying to get through to attack the Arctic convoy JW55B was the last battle of World War II in which a British battleship was involved. After the *Scharnhorst* had been hit by torpedoes from three British destroyers, the battleship *Duke of York* fired her guns from close range and sank the German ship.

HMS Duke of York **in her prime, serving with the Home Fleet in 1949**

HMS Duke of York **comes alongside the quay at the end of her last voyage to the breakers in 1958**

HMS Vanguard **firing a salvo from her 15-inch guns. Her flared forecastle made her a magnificent sea-boat. The last and best of the long line of British battleships, she carried the most comprehensive outfit of AA guns: no fewer than 72 Bofors guns, most of which were in six-barrelled radar-controlled mountings.**

One of the four King George V class battleships, *HMS Anson*, leaving the Gare Loch on the Clyde in 1958, bound for the scrap-yard. Two years later, she would be followed by the *Vanguard*

Conclusion

Ships are the biggest mobile structures on earth and, to this status, the battleship added another dimension. They had to stay afloat in the face of attacks from torpedoes, air bombing, mines and shells. In addition, they had to withstand the tremendous shock of firing their own ordnance, as well as provide a home for her crew. The battleship dominated the oceans for less than a century, but left a magnificent legacy of action and power. We shall not see their like again.

***HMS Anson*, 1945**

***HMS Barham*, 1934**

***HMS Nelson*, 1942**

***HMS Prince of Wales*, 1941**

***HMS Queen Elizabeth*, 1943**

HMS Repulse

HMS Vanguard

***HMS Warspite*, 1937**